FOREVER FAITHFUL

Forever Faithful: Miraculous Stories of God's Faithfulness to a Praying Wife and Mother

Copyright © 2018 Stephanie Lombardo

Scriptures taken from the Holy Bible, New International Version®, NIV®. Copyright © 1973, 1978, 1984, 2011 by Biblica, Inc.™ Used by permission of Zondervan. All rights reserved worldwide. www.zondervan.com The "NIV" and "New International Version" are trademarks registered in the United States Patent and Trademark Office by Biblica, Inc.™

"Scripture quotations taken from the Amplified® Bible (AMP), Copyright © 2015 by The Lockman Foundation. Used by permission. www.Lockman.org"

ISBN: 9781797563497

PULPIT TO PAGE PUBLISHING CO. BOOKS MAY BE ORDERED THROUGH BOOKSELLERS OR BY CONTACTING:

PTP PUBLISHING CO. || USA & ABROAD

PULPITTOPAGE.COM

FOREVER FAITHFUL

MIRACULOUS STORIES OF GOD'S FAITHFULNESS
TO A PRAYING WIFE AND MOTHER

STEPHANIE LOMBARDO

"I am so proud of my mother and her faithfulness to chronicle the Lord's goodness in her life and the life of her family and friends. I know it hasn't been an easy journey, but I've seen the reward of the Lord in her life before my very eyes. Because of her, faith has continued in our family line and continues to grow. I was raised hearing stories of God's power and grace. It marked me from a young age. Her steadfastness in prayer, boldness in proclamation and the compassion and mercy she wears as a garment is inspiring, challenging, and points those that meet her right to Jesus. I'm so proud of her and I know this book will impact many hearts for the kingdom. Love you mom! Because of you, I am who I am today. You've made a bigger difference than you can possibly fathom."

—**MICHAEL LOMBARDO**, Minister, Host of Awaken Live and Author of *Immersed in His Glory*, *lifepouredoutintl.org*

"Stephanie Lombardo's story is not only inspirational and motivational, but it is also transformational. I pray the Lord uses it, not only in your life, but in the lives of your family members and friends. Be sure to share this book with everyone you know who needs hope, healing, and a new beginning."

—**PASTOR JOHN J. WAGNER**, Pastor of *Epic Church International,* Sayreville, NJ

"Stephanie Lombardo's stories of remarkable faith, resilience and answers to prayer will stir up hope inside of you no matter what you may be facing in your life. The Bible reminds us that we overcome "by the word of our testimony!" If you want to overcome, this is for you. This is a book of very compelling testimonies of a praying wife, mother, and friend who has lived a life of answered prayer! These prayer victories will leave you saying *why not me?* This book of real life God inspired stories will strengthen you, encourage you and give you hope in a good God no matter what you may be going through! This book is a must read!"

—**JOE FORTUNATO**, Pastor, *Faith Fellowship Ministries of South Jersey*, Founder of *South Jersey Dream Center*

"I have had the pleasure of knowing Stephanie for many years. Since the first time my husband and I met her, she has always proven to be a strong, kind, prayerful woman of God. I feel that anyone who reads this book will be given the opportunity to truly see what it means to trust God in every area of your life. Through time and time again she overcame obstacles with unwavering faith and trust in God which only attends to her resisting opportunities to accept defeat in her family's lives. I pray that this book ministers to those who read it and shows the greatness of our God and the amazingly godly example in Stephanie. The Lombardo Family hold a dear place in my heart as they were always faithful to our Church and my husband and I. Congratulations on a beautiful book Stephanie. May God bless you in abundance for blessing so many others."

—DIANE DeMOLA

"Let me encourage you to pick up a copy of this very encouraging and uplifting read for yourself and others. It addresses the heart issues of those who might be struggling for peace in the midst of life's trials and troubles. You'll find yourself captivated by the down to earth, honest and real life testimonies of one woman who dared to believe God against all odds. Through her everyday struggles she will teach you how to lay hold of God and His promises so that you too can watch Him work in the midst of your darkest hour. And not only that, you'll discover the secrets to accessing God's miracle working power that's available to all who believe!"

—CANDICE SIMMONS, *thepassiontranslation.com*

"FAITH! It perfectly describes Stephanie. This book will have you on a journey of faith and trust. Faith in that we can trust God not only for outcomes, but in the journey. Stephanie gives us tools and inspiration to continue to walk in faith while the promise is still in progress. Her faith is most tangible by its fruit-loving family and friends that

serve God as a result of her faith. I cried, and I cried again.
I am provoked to believe for more."

—GABRIEL ZAMORA, Zamora Ministries

"We all need encouragement along our journey of faith,
so getting to read about the real life struggles of a relatable
person is really helpful! I'd strongly encourage you to read
Stephanie's book, as I think it will encourage your faith!"

—SARAH BOWLING, Founder of *Saving Moses,* Co-host
of *Marilyn and Sarah, savingmoses.org*

I dedicate this book to my wonderful husband and the love of my life. I'm so grateful that God put us together so many years ago and with His grace, kept us together, through thick and thin. And our love is stronger than ever.

Joe, you are a man after God's own heart, who would do anything for your family. You work hard for us, you love us so well, and you still make me laugh.... a lot! You love and serve God with all your heart! I love you Joe with all of mine!

ACKNOWLEDGMENTS

To our wonderful kids, Joseph, Danielle, Michelle and Michael. You are all precious gifts from God that Dad and I have had the privilege and joy of loving and watching you all grow into the amazing adults that you are. All so gifted in your unique ways and the most rewarding for us is that you all love the Lord with all your hearts. You have all chosen wonderful spouses, Rene, Teresa and Selina, whom we love as our own and it is the joy of our hearts to watch you all loving each other and loving and serving God with all your hearts, and raising our wonderful grandchildren to do the same. What more could me and Dad ask for? We love you all beyond words and are filled with such gratitude to God for you all!

And Michael, I thank you also for all your encouragement and help in the process of making this book a reality. There were times I wasn't so sure it would ever really happen. You'd always ask me how the book was coming and then used your experience to help me in many ways. Thank you.

To all our amazing grandkids, Joey, Johny, Anthony, Chiara, Isabelle, Gabriella, Selah, Nico and Jude. There are no adequate words to describe the joy each one of you have given Grandpa and me. You are all so loving, smart and talented in so many ways. And hysterical! God has truly blessed us and we are so grateful. We love you all with all our hearts.

To my sister in law, Angela. I've known you for going on 51 years and you've made me laugh for all 51. You're such a blessing to the whole family. Anyone of us know that if we need you in any way, whether it's prayer support or anything at all, you'll be there. We appreciate you so much and love you with all our hearts.

To my siblings, Steve, Sue and Chris. I'm so thankful that we've always been so close and have always tried to be there for each other, no matter what the need. You've given me two wonderful nephews, J.J. and Frankie and a wonderful niece, Rachel. I love and appreciate you all so much.

And my baby brother, Frank, whose untimely death at the age of 18, though it was a heartbreaking time for all of us, one by one, it brought us all into the arms of Jesus and He healed our broken hearts in time and gave us new life in Him. I'm so grateful to God, who takes our heartbreaks and tragedies and heals us and brings good out of them. He saved us and gave us a new life we never knew existed or could have imagined with our Savior.

And to Pastor Joe Fortunato and Natalie, who, after sharing with them some of my testimony, were the first to encourage me to write this book. Thank you for your encouragement and love.

And most importantly, to my Lord, Who has always done immeasurably more than I have ever asked or imagined in my life and my family's lives. You are the exceedingly, abundant God. No praise could ever be enough! You have been everything to me and always will be. You truly have always been and will always be Forever Faithful. Your Name be praised forever!!!

CONTENTS

"But as for me, it is good to be near God. I have made the Sovereign Lord my refuge; I will tell of all your deeds."

— PSALM 73:28

INTRODUCTION

As I've read and reread these chapters that I have written, the one recurring thread in each of these testimonies is *trust*. Trusting God. He is so worthy of our trust. Sometimes it can be so hard to see past our circumstances. You wonder, "How will God get me through this?" I've been there! In those times, sometimes all you can do, through tears, is say, "I trust you Lord", or "I know you love my family member more than I do". Or, "You're faithful Lord" or "You promised Father!" I've said them all. I've cried buckets of tears, but God was always there to lift me up as I worshipped Him and recounted His promises. I've spent countless hours on my knees over the last 43 years, where I found God waiting. And there it was that I was comforted, that I was taught by Him and was strengthened by His love. It was there that I experienced the supernatural *peace that passes all understanding.* In those precious times alone with God, He heard me and comforted me and always gave me what I needed to hold on. Just knowing that God loved me and my family, that I could run to Him any time of the day or night and He would be there with open ears and arms, held me together and filled me with hope.

Whether it's spending time with Him, whether it is pouring out our heart in tears, or worshipping Him while remembering His glorious promises for us, or just being silent before Him... He's there in it all! So many times I've run to my prayer closet, anxious and in tears, and come out with His peace. In the midst of the storm there can be a beautiful peace, if we run to our wonderful Heavenly Father. He is our only help and comfort! He is our only Hope, our Strength, our Joy. He is our Healer, our Savior, our King. I truly don't remember ever getting angry at God or blaming Him for the difficult circumstances in my life. Things that seemed impossible and took many years to see answered. I clung to God for dear life and believed He was a Promise Keeper. I look back on those times and, although I would never want to go through them again, I see that as I clung to God, He taught me and changed me the most in those difficult times. In those times I experienced His nearness and love and faithfulness in ways I never would have, if my life had been pain free. We all have had, or will have, things in our lives that are hard and very painful, but God promises never to leave us or forsake us. And He won't! One of my favorite Scriptures is John 16:33. It reads, "In this world you will have trouble, but take heart, I have overcome the world." And His Word also says that we are *more than conquerors through Christ*. Not in our own strength, but *through Christ*. (Romans 8:36)

If you were to ask me to tell you what one of the most valuable lessons I've learned in my Christian walk over the last 43 years is, I would say that no matter how difficult or long or painful the situation is, our *trust in God* has brought me and my family through it all. *Trusting in His limitless love and His Word, that can never fail.*

It is my prayer that as you read the chapters of this book, that you will be encouraged. And that if you are struggling in a situation that has your faith severely tested and you are hanging on by only a thread of faith, like I have been at various times, be encouraged. God hears your cries and sees your tears and honors your faith. No matter how weak it may seem at the time. Be weak before Him, because that is when He is so strong. Worship Him in those times, when it seems like nothing is going right and it is so difficult. You can't see any way through. Praise Him anyway! He inhabits our praise! That *sacrifice of praise* is so much more precious to God than when we praise Him when everything is rosy. How pleased His heart must be when He hears our praise through heartbroken tears! I've been there and God has blessed my tears with a peace that I did not have before I ran to Him. In our weakness, He is strong. (2 Corinthians 12:9-10) He is able. And what He's done for me and my family, He'll do for you.

In no way am I saying that our lives are now struggle-free. That would be nice, but only when we see His glorious face will all struggles cease. However, after all these years, we have a long history with God and He's never let us down. It may not always turn out our way, or in our timing, but God's way is always the best way and He is never late! And He'll always give us what we need to go through to the other side, as He teaches and changes us. All He asks of us is to BELIEVE.

MY SALVATION STORY

$\mathcal{I}$n May of 1974, Memorial Day weekend, while I was experiencing the joys of being a new mother to my 7 month old son, tragedy struck my family! My baby brother, who had just turned eighteen a month earlier, had drowned while visiting Florida with his best friend for the holiday weekend. At that time, the legal drinking age was eighteen and Frankie and his friend took advantage of and abused this law that weekend. Their car broke down on the way home from bar hopping and my brother, who was in no condition to make a rational decision, decided to swim across the body of water that supposedly separated them from his friends' father's home. His friend stayed behind to get help for his car. His friend lived. When my family got the news it was unbearable. It couldn't be true! But it was true. We were all devastated, but my

Mother was destroyed. A parent's' worst nightmare...losing a child.

Frank was the third of five children. I am the second in line and oldest daughter. He was four years younger, his whole life was ahead of him, but cut so short by the terrible choices he made. My siblings and I took the responsibility of holding our mother together, because she was so broken. Unfortunately, my Father was suffering terribly as we all were and he wasn't much help to her, so I tried my best to help. My little son was a great distraction. Children bring such joy, but my mother was so hurt and angry. She felt betrayed by God. We grew up Catholic. My mom stopped going to church and refused to even speak to a priest for almost a year. I visited her with my son as often as I could and called her every night. She was in terrible shape. It was heartbreaking to see your mother so hurt and trying to deal with your own heartache and grief at the same time.

Finally my aunt, mom's sister, got her to go to a Charismatic Catholic Church. They had a prayer meeting every week and she started attending. She received Jesus Christ as her Lord and Savior and was Baptized by the Holy Spirit. She would tell me all about these meetings and about being "Born Again", a term I'd never heard before. She said God had given her peace about Frankie. She had a new life in Christ and she told me I needed this new life too. We spoke every night and she told me things that were so new to me and hard to understand. But I knew one thing was true. My mom was changed and at peace. It was a miracle! God healed her broken heart and gave her new life and she wanted that for me too, so although I didn't understand many of the things she told me, I wanted what she had.

In October of 1975, they had another Life in the Spirit Seminar. My mother said that if I attended it I could receive Christ and be *born again*. I decided that if this could make such a difference in my mother's life, it must be good for me too. I went that first night and I felt a peace that I had never experienced before in my life. I felt like I never wanted to leave that room. I only later understood that this peace was what God promises in the Bible. The peace that passes all understanding. [Philippians 4:7] Since then I've experienced it many times over the years. A peace the world can't give. God's peace. It was overwhelming.

That October I got born again and Baptized by the Holy Spirit and my life has never been the same! Even though my brother died tragically, his death brought my whole family, one by one, to a new life in Jesus Christ. One we never knew we could have, or even knew existed. That was forty three years ago and I thank God with all my heart for saving me when He did. In life there are many challenges and heartaches, as well as joys. I can't even imagine what my life would have been like without my relationship with God. He's been there and brought me and my family through all that life has brought our way. My gratitude to God is much greater than words could ever express. God is so good and so faithful.

GOD CAN GET US THROUGH ANYTHING

(FIRST MISCARRIAGE)

*I*t was the spring of 1980, in the month of April. I was pregnant with our third child. We were expecting and thrilled. I was in my third month and feeling great! I never even had a day of morning sickness in any of my pregnancies. Being in my third month and already having had two children, I was beginning to show.

It was Good Friday and I was preparing to have the family over for Easter dinner. I was excited to celebrate the Resurrection of our Lord with all my family. At some point that morning, I went to the bathroom and to my horror, there was blood in my urine! That was not normal for me. I was so scared! I immediately started crying out to God! I pulled myself together and brought my two young children to my mother's house so that I could get to the doctor's office. The doctor told me that I needed total bed rest in the hopes of saving our baby.

How could this be happening to me? I was a Christian and believed God could do anything! Well, I needed Him now and told Him exactly what I expected and fully believed that He could do! Fix me and the baby! Simple for Him, right?! Well, my mother had come home with me so that she could care for the kids and I could rest. We prayed together and I laid down. I only got up to go to the bathroom. While I lay on the couch, I read a great book, that day and the next. It really helped to bolster my faith, until I got up to go to the bathroom. Everytime my hopes were dashed by the blood I saw mixed with urine. I kept demanding that God save my child, through heartbroken tears. This went on all Friday until early Saturday evening. I was on an emotional roller coaster! After dinner Saturday night, I felt cramping and I was very scared. Mom prayed with me and I went up to bed. As I lay there, I realized that this wasn't going my way. I had demanded my child's healing, but it wasn't happening, At least not the way I expected or wanted. I finally came to the place of surrender. I stopped telling God what He had to do. Through humble tears I told God in those moments that it was ok if He allowed this to happen. I told Him that I believed that He knew what was best for me and the baby and that I would love and praise Him, no matter what the outcome.

I lost that child but God was so amazing to me through it. It was one of those times that I experienced the peace that passes all understanding, that He promises. (Philippians 4;7) This was such a heartbreaking thing for me and my husband, but in the middle of this raging storm, after I put the baby and myself in God's hands, my heart was completely at peace, knowing my God was with us and would get us through this. Loving and comforting scriptures that I had hidden in my heart since giving my heart to God, were floating around in my head. In the emergency room, I was actually humming and singing softly to myself and praying for my husband because he was a wreck. I wished so much that I could share this amazing, unexplainable peace, with him. God was with me through the D & C procedure that I needed. I had such peace, it was amazing. A complete 180 degree turn from my state of mind on Friday and Saturday. Because I was so at peace, I refused the sedative the nurse offered me. That would have helped me through the epidural they had to give me before the procedure. I didn't even think of that. I just knew I was in God's hands, and it was Him that got me through it. I never had that "why me" aftermath. God had completely healed me, in His way!

After waiting three months to heal up, I got pregnant again. I had a beautiful pregnancy and exactly one year from that miscarriage, the following Good

Friday, God gave us a beautiful baby girl! When I looked at the clock as I was being rolled into the delivery room and saw that it was 11:30 pm, Good Friday, and I realized what God had done, I wept for joy. Tears were rolling into my ears! My God is so good and so faithful! Though the loss of that child was so heartbreaking to me, God was with me so lovingly, and through this experience healed me and showed me how good and how near and how faithful He is in the most difficult times of our lives. I look back on this time as a time where I got to know God so much more intimately. I experienced His peace, and love and faithfulness in a way I never had before. And God is such a wonderful Father. He understood when I was fighting so hard and ordering Him around, telling Him exactly what I wanted and how. He saw my pain and understood and lovingly brought me to a place where I could surrender all that hurt and all those tears, and just trust that His way was always the right way, always the perfect way. The Bible says in Romans 8:28 that "All things work together for good, for those who love God and are the called according to His purpose." Although it was a very hard time for me to go through, losing that child, I know that baby is with the Lord and that someday we'll all be together. I look back on that time as a blessing that brought me nearer to God. God is so faithful and with all my heart I am so grateful.

OUR PRODIGAL SON

*I*t was in 2004, about 7:30 in the morning. As was my habit, I got up and made breakfast for my sixteen year old son, Michael. Always the same. A peanut butter and jelly sandwich. To this day he still loves pb & j sandwiches, and he's 31 now! I'd make the sandwich and read my Bible and pray and watch some morning Christian programs to start my day. This morning was no different, except that Michael was running a little late that day. Michael was in a punk band and had just started gluing and spiking up his beautiful thick, curly black hair. It was so thick that it was quite an undertaking, hence he was running very late and rushing. He sat across from me on the arm of the chair, hurriedly putting his sneakers on! I looked at him and teased him about having to get up earlier now so that he could glue up his hair. Well,

Michael wasn't a morning person to begin with, and he was in a rush and not in the mood for my teasing at all! He looked at me so angrily and said something so mean, I could hardly register the words that impaled my heart. My eyes must have shut with the impact of his words. When I opened them, Michael was gone. I just sat there on the couch, Bible closed on my lap, weeping uncontrollably. Where had my precious son gone? It seemed like just yesterday he was still telling me I was the most beautiful mommy . Always so loving and affectionate. What happened? I asked God through my tears, how this could have happened to my beautiful son? How could such an angry, ugly thing come out of his mouth at all? *But to say it to me*?

You see, Michael had begun a rebellious, troubled journey, starting from about age 14. It started like most teenagers with the back talk and rebelling against the rules. He had been an A student. He was funny and smart and lovable, just to name a few traits. He was never any problem. But, he met some boys in high school who influenced his life very negatively. And even though he grew up in a Christian home with a very loving family and all he ever needed, he got on the wrong path, and it grew darker with each year that passed, until he could look at his Mother, who he truly loved, and say words I never thought I would hear from him. Well, he did come to me after school and apologize. He was truly sorry and I knew it. He had a beautiful, loving heart. It was just slowly getting covered over with the junk of the influences he chose to spend his time with. Of course he was grounded, and it was amazing how when Michael was away from his friends for a week, we had our Michael back.

Getting back to the part of the story where I was left sitting on the couch brokenhearted. I don't know how long I sat there weeping. Crying out to God! Finally I calmed myself and dried my tears. I couldn't just sit there all day weeping and feeling sorry for myself. I glanced at the closed Bible on my lap and said, "God, where do I read now?" I heard no answer, but just opened it with my left hand and as I did, some pages softly turned until the pages remained still and the Bible remained open. I looked down to see that it was opened to a Book in the Old Testament. It was Jeremiah, chapter 31, and my eyes focused on verses 16 and 17.

It read, "Thus says the Lord; refrain your voice from weeping, and your eyes from tears; For your work will be rewarded, says the Lord. And they shall come back from the land of the enemy. There is a hope in your future, says the Lord, that your children shall come back to their own border." Well, as you can imagine, I was weeping all over again! In those moments, God gave me a much deeper awareness of His nearness. In my pain, He was there. So close. He saw me! He heard me! He answered me and gave me hope and a promise to cling to in the moments I would need it. And there would be many moments of weakness and tears and trusting God, while waiting for the manifestation of that promise He gave to me for our son. It was another four years before Michael came to the end of himself and cried out to God. So much happened in those years, but God had given me a promise, and oh, *He is a Promise Keeper*!

Today, ten years later, Michael is a minister of the Gospel of Jesus Christ. He spent a year home after his last car accident, that surely would have killed him, except for the mercy and faithfulness of God. Michael came away with only a couple of scratches on his arm. A true miracle! This accident that could have taken his life, instead brought him to his knees. He knew that God had spared his life and in his desperation, he cried out to God. He was at the end of himself. He told God that if He could do something with the life he had messed up so badly the last six years, that he would serve Him for the rest of his life. Well, God showed up and kept His promise to me. Michael's life changed from that moment on and he was filled with a burning love for God. He started back at church and a year later God called him to Dallas, to attend Christ for the Nations Institute, a well-known Bible and Mission training School. He spent three years there and has traveled all over the world with CFNI since, doing mission work and preaching the Gospel, ministering to the poorest of the poor. Bringing the love of God to those who so desperately need it. But then, we all desperately need it. This wonderful, life transforming, glorious love of God. The same God that Michael had turned away from for six years, had welcomed him back into His arms, just like the prodigal in the Bible. God delivered Michael from drugs and alcohol addiction, healed his heart and mind, and filled him with so much love and gratitude to God, that his life for the last ten years has been poured out for Jesus. God has more than fulfilled His promise to me and answered the prayers of our whole family for him. He takes our sorrow and turns it into joy. He only asks us to *believe*! And He is there every step of the way, strengthening us, teaching us, comforting us and giving us what we need to get us through to the other side. A victory we couldn't even have imagined in our finite minds. He truly is the exceedingly abundant God. (Ephesians 3;20) Praise His Holy name!

Michael's story, of which I've only shared a fraction, has been an inspiration and an encouragement to countless people. Young and old. God brings us through the worst problems of our lives. In Michael's case, it was a six year journey down a dark road and for us who loved him with all our hearts, it was so difficult to watch and many tears were shed. But more importantly, many prayers were said. No matter how hard, we never gave up on our beautiful son. We stood on God's

Word for him. There is nothing more powerful than the Word of God. The Apostle Paul said that we should speak those things that be not, as though they are. (Romans 4:17) We spoke what we knew God saw in Michael. That is my advice to anyone who is praying for a loved one, no matter the circumstance. No matter what you see in the natural, speak and agree with what God says. Though many times it will be through tears, brush them aside and open your mouth and speak the glorious, powerful Word of God. The Word that is alive and never changing and never failing. Agree with God in your situation. God is so faithful! How well I know that. When the victory comes, we have a glorious testimony from our pain, that we can now share with others who are in pain and going through hard situations, maybe even the same type of trial that you've been brought through. Our past pain then becomes a gift we can now give away, to help others through theirs.

Michael could have been dead, more than once, but God miraculously protected him, and today the life and love of Christ emanates from him. Today Michael is in part time ministry, preaching and teaching the Gospel and love of Jesus Christ. He's been all over the world doing missions work and as a matter of fact, he met his wife in Africa while they were both serving the poor together. He and his beautiful wife have a beautiful baby girl and boy, whose lives light up our lives, as all our grandkids do. He teaches in the Bible school at our church on occasion and travels to churches all over the country preaching and teaching and blessing the lives of many. He's even published a book which is full of his testimony and what God has taught him over the last ten years. It is so amazing! Truly a miracle. The greatest miracle of all, *a completely changed heart and life.*

Nothing is impossible for God! Keep believing for yourself, your loved ones, your finances, whatever. God is faithful and he loves you and your loved ones with an everlasting love. The road may sometimes be very difficult to travel, but if you have Jesus, you never travel it alone.

HE TURNED MY ASHES TO JOY

(MY SECOND MISCARRIAGE)

*I*n June of 1986, I suffered my second miscarriage. The first one was in 1980, after which, one year exactly to the day of that miscarriage, God blessed us with a beautiful baby girl. Through that heartbreak, God showed Himself to be so near and so faithful to me. What was so devastating to me, God turned into joy and strengthened my faith dramatically as He brought me through this very difficult time, with such love. Just six years later, in the month of June, on my birthday, to be exact, I miscarried another precious baby. My husband and I had only just a few days before, celebrated the news that we were expecting our fourth child. What a birthday present. Needless to say, we were very upset! We were so excited about our new baby coming because we had waited longer to try for this child, because our third was such a handful and I didn't feel ready. Until now. As soon as we decided to try, we became pregnant almost immediately. It was awesome news. But no sooner had we celebrated the wonderful news, we were devastated with the possibility of losing another child. I immediately made a doctor's appointment for later that morning. Well , you know the drill when you go to any doctor's office. Even when you have an appointment, you most likely wait. So I waited. Me and my thoughts, on my birthday. After a while they called me into the examining room where I would continue to wait. As I waited, I remember sitting on the edge of the examination table, crying, wondering why this had happened to me again. I remember telling the Lord that this was the worst birthday imaginable. But in my heart I knew that next year on my birthday, God was going to do something special for me. I knew it in my heart because of what He did after my first miscarriage.

I didn't suffer terribly, like I did the first time because I remembered the goodness of the Lord. I lost a baby six years ago on Good Friday and God gave me another beautiful child on the following Good Friday, and completely healed my broken heart. God is so amazing and faithful! So now as I sat and waited for the doctor, I remembered , and trusted God for a beautiful birthday the following year. I believed in God's goodness and told Him so.

It didn't play out exactly as it had the first time. I

didn't have a new baby in my arms on my next birthday, but I took a pregnancy test that day and it was positive!!!! I knew it! What I believed in my heart, God brought to pass. The news of new life coming. On my birthday! We were filled with joy and celebrated the goodness of God in our lives and nine months later, we had a precious, beautiful baby boy in our arms. Praise God! He takes the sorrow and turns it into joy if we just trust Him. (Psalm 30:11) He comforts, and strengthens and teaches us in the midst of the worst times of our lives, if we let Him. It is in these times that we truly come to know the faithfulness and steadfast love of our Heavenly Father. He Gives us a peace that surpasses all understanding, just like He promises in His Word. I'm so grateful. God is so good!

THE COMB

$\mathcal{W}$hen I was five years old I had the experience that I'm about to relay. I remember it as if it happened yesterday, even though it happened 60 years ago. This experience made a deep impact on me as a little girl that would stay with me all these many years, as it cemented my faith in God. No matter how I strayed from church as a teenager, up until I was 23 and accepted Jesus Christ as my Savior, no one would ever be able to convince me that there was not a God, Who not only heard, but answered a little girl's prayer.

One morning I stood in front of my mother's dressing table, combing my almost waist length hair, with my mother's comb. This comb was a thick, pink plastic comb, six or eight inches in length. There was absolutely no bending or breaking this comb. For some silly reason, I took a section of my hair right on the top of my head and raised my little arms up, with hair and comb in hand. I pulled my hair up as high as my little arms could reach and wrapped the end of my hair around it, and with both hands, each holding one end of the comb, began winding the comb downward to the top of my head. I'm sure you're getting the picture. I didn't realize the consequences to that action until I tried to take it out. What a surprise to my young mind when it wouldn't obey. I struggled for a few minutes, to no avail, and after failing miserably, I decided to go to mom. She could do it! *Mom could do anything!* Well, not quite this time. I wonder what my mom thought as I walked towards her, resembling Pebbles Flintstone, with that long comb stuck to the top of my head. She chuckled a little at first, not realizing what she was in for. Very patiently she started working on disentangling my hair from the comb. She tried for quite a while, as the comb would not obey her either. I don't know exactly how long. It sure seemed like forever! She started to tell me, as she was getting frustrated with this comb, that she was going to have to cut it out of my hair!!! Even at that young age, I knew that was not good. I immediately started crying, begging my mother to please keep trying and not cut my hair!! My mother took pity on her very upset little girl and kept trying. She tried and tried and *tried* until all her trying had now caused this comb to be so firmly lodged in my hair, that it now wouldn't budge. It was far worse than when she began. I was wailing from the thought of my hair being cut and from the pain this whole procedure had inflicted upon me! My poor mother got so exasperated, she just threw her arms up in the air and said, " Oh Steffie, just go in your room and pray to God that we get this comb out of your hair!"

So, that's exactly what I did. I remember getting on my knees at my bedside, with folded hands and head bowed, crying, asking God to please get this comb out of my hair or mommy was going to have to cut it out!! Might sound silly to some, but it wasn't to me, or to God. He loves it when we come to Him with child-like faith. Somehow He gave me the grace to believe that if I went to Him, like mommy said, He would help me. I don't know how many minutes went by, but when I was done I went and found my mom. When I stood in front of her, with my little hopeful, tear-stained face, my mother reached out and took one end of the comb in her hand, and she pulled it right out! There was no resistance! The comb came right out! One little tug and I was free!! Every hair on my cute little head intact! It was amazing! A miracle! God listened to a little girl's prayer, my prayer, and He cared. And He answered. I've imagined the God of all creation, looking down at me pouring out my heart, and His heart was moved. What a wonderful God! From that moment I believed. I've told my little miracle story countless times over the years and it's been a blessing to those I've shared it with. I thank God for that experience, because it cemented my faith in His love, and that He lives and His ears are open to our cries. And He's so eager to answer. Praise Him.

That is the first that I remember over the years. First of many answered prayers and miracles that I'm sharing in this book. But I believe it was that experience with my Heavenly Father, that instilled deep in my heart, that no matter what happened in the years to come, I always had my wonderful God to run to, and He would be there waiting to catch me in His arms. I'm so grateful!

THE ACID THAT DIDN'T BURN

*O*ne freezing, winter morning many years ago, I was sitting in my family room, having my prayer time with the Lord. It was early. About eight a.m.. My two young children were still asleep as they usually were at that time, and it was my time in the quiet and peace of the morning to be with God. I would read my Bible and pray for my loved ones and whatever concerns I might have. Well, as I began to pray for my husband, Joe, I couldn't stop. I can only explain the feeling I had as *an urgency within me to pray for my husband's protection.* He had been at work by now, for at least an hour or so. I had no reason to believe that he was in any danger, but I was sure praying like he was! I prayed urgently for him for a few minutes. I don't even know how long, but I finally felt a release somehow and stopped. I don't know how else to describe it. I had never had that experience prior to that morning and I don't think I have since in that same way. I remember thinking how strange that was to me. Praying that way, like I had no control over that prayer at all. I couldn't stop until I was done. Although I knew it was strange, I put it behind me and finished my prayer time and went on with my very busy day. Two small children make for a very busy day!

My husband finally came home that evening and as he walked into the room where I was, the first words out of his mouth were, and I quote, "Oh my God, Stephanie, I almost got killed today!" I immediately asked him what happened, not even remembering yet my experience that morning. As I listened to his story, I stood speechless, trying to take it in.

This is what he told me. But I must just back up a little bit to give you the background of what had happened. My husband was and still is a contractor and worked outside, most of the time. This particular morning was frigid, but the work had to be done. Unfortunately, a truck that was needed that morning, wouldn't start. The battery was frozen! Trying to get it started, Joe lifted the hood of the truck and started checking everything. He connected cables to the battery to jump it while someone else was in the truck, cranking the ignition key.

While my husband was bent under that truck hood, the battery exploded and metal and battery acid flew everywhere! Joe was covered with the battery acid as pieces of shattered metal flew everywhere! He told me that it blew on his face and landed all over him. Now, I'm listening to him and looking at him incredulously, because I know that acid burns! He said it went on his face, but his face was perfect! Then my eyes traveled to his jacket and down to his jeans and what I saw amazed me and jogged my memory concerning my morning experience. His jacket had big holes in it! And so did his jeans! Yet the acid did not burn his skin. Acid would not have just stopped at the fabric, it would have continued to burn through his skin. And what about his face? Not a mark! I think if I hadn't seen the shape of his jacket and jeans I might have wondered if he was stretching the truth a bit!

My mind was racing as I was trying to take in what I was seeing. I think the color was leaving my face because my husband now asked what was wrong with me? All I could say was to ask what time this had happened? He said that it was the exact time that I had been praying for him. I told him about my experience that morning and he was as amazed as me and very grateful. He had no trouble believing that God had supernaturally protected him, because he had been that target underneath that truck hood. He knew he should have been in the hospital that night, not home, perfectly whole, relaying this miracle of God's Grace to me. It would be at least another twenty years before my husband asked Jesus to be his Savior, but that miracle was something he would never forget. One of many over the next few decades, until now. God is the same yesterday, today and forever. (Hebrews 13:8) If we will just put our trust in Him, He will never leave us or forsake us. Sometimes we don't even understand what's happening in a moment until later. I've learned that God works in many, many ways. If we make ourselves available to Him in our quiet times, we can hear Him, or be moved by Holy Spirit to pray for a loved one, like I was. I'll never forget that morning. Nor will my husband. Over the last 43 years since I've committed my life to Jesus, He has been so faithful to my family and I, and I thank Him with all of my heart.

THE FIRE OF 2001

*I*t was a beautiful Saturday afternoon! Not a cloud in the sky. A little breezy, but just perfect! I remember distinctly praising God for such a glorious day. You know, one of those days you wish we could have every day of the year. I know most of us have said that at one time or another. Yes, it was beautiful, but I had no idea what was about to unfold.

My youngest son, Michael had his friend over that day. Michael asked if I could go get some lunch for them at the nearby fast food joint. I agreed and was gone for about 20 minutes. When I got back home I remember getting out of my car and immediately smelling smoke. I thought to myself that I should call the Fire Department, but no sooner had I thought it, I heard the fire sirens sound! Twenty four years earlier, there was a fire in the woods surrounding our property and it got pretty bad, but God saved our home and property. The Fire Department was wonderful and God gave them the grace to get the job done. So when I heard the sirens blaring, I knew that the Fire Department was already on the way to wherever that smell of smoke was coming from. Unfortunately, it smelled suspiciously close. With that thought, I went inside to bring the kids their lunch and forgot about it until about a half an hour later. My daughter, Danielle, called me to look out of our study window at the front of the house. To my surprise and slight discomfort, I saw the Fire truck that she was pointing at. It was parked right in our driveway! Oh my goodness! Here we go again! I went outside to ask the Firemen what was happening? They pointed to the back corner of our property, about 200 feet or so behind our house in the woods. What I saw is hard to describe, but it looked like a swirling tornado with fire shooting out of it! It was an extremely breezy day and it had been very dry for some time, so the fire was being well fed and well spread by the dry trees and the strong breeze.

Well, I went back into the house and told the kids, who were pretty nervous by now, to stay inside. I told them that everything would be alright. The firemen were on the job, and most importantly that God would protect us. I went upstairs to the back corner bedroom and looked out the window to get a different perspective of what was happening. It wasn't good, but as I looked at this ominous, fire filled tornado, I spoke to God and told Him I trusted Him. When I was a very young Christian, not many years before the first fire, I discovered Psalm 91 in the Bible during my prayer time. It was so amazing and such a comfort, that I put it to memory. Verses 10 and 11 in my Bible read, "No disaster shall overtake you, nor any plague come near you, for He has placed you in His angels charge, to guard you wherever you go." Well, during the first fire, I recited those promises of Psalm 91 and told God that I trusted Him and He kept His promise. He saved our home. So as I looked out the same window, I had no doubt that we were in good hands, no matter how bad it looked! And it looked pretty bad, but I had a peace in my heart that the Bible promises in Philippians 4:7. And as the next few hours unfolded, I was blessed with His amazing peace. And boy would I need it. This fire turned out to be far more serious than that first one was years ago!

A few minutes later the firemen were at the door telling us that we had to evacuate our home because of the danger surrounding the house. Our house was being totally covered with dense smoke and strips of ash were falling from the sky everywhere. They told us that we had to go up the street, while they fought the fire. I gathered the three pretty frightened kids, and grabbed my purse and phone, and was about to follow them out the door when I paused. The devil put a thought in my head to gather up some family photos, just in case. You see those were the things that I would most hate losing. My memories. The devil loves to plant those seeds of doubt and fear in our minds. That's where our greatest battles are. In our minds. But my next thought came from my hope and trust in God, who I knew to be faithful. I thought, "No, I trust you Lord! I'm not going to grab any pictures, just in case. I either trust You or I don't."

We left the house and we walked up the street. My son's friend's mom came to pick the boys up to bring them to their house during this ordeal. She couldn't drive down the street because of all the fire trucks and volunteers that had gathered, not to mention all of us who got evacuated from our homes. She walked down to meet us and took the boys home with her. But before Michael, who was 12 at the time, left with his friend, he looked at me with tears in his eyes, and asked, "Mom, are we going to lose everything?" By that time, our house was barely visible and the ash was falling everywhere and covering the street. I've never experienced anything like that before and hope never to again. My heart broke as I looked into my sons eyes, but with the grace of God, I was able to tell him, with a sure conviction and peace in my heart, that he shouldn't worry. I told him that when he got home later, that our house would be there. I was able to calm his fears. Only by *God's grace*. That *supernatural peace* that Philippians talks about. A peace the world can't give or understand. There was no earthly reason that I should have been at peace then, or for the next few hours as the firefighters fought to save our home. A couple of my neighbors came over to me, with expressions of great sympathy, and asked me how I was doing. They fully expected that when the smoke lifted, my home would be gone for sure, and wondered if the firemen could possibly save theirs. But, the amazing thing is that I was able to encourage them! You couldn't see my house for the smoke, but I knew that when the smoke cleared, our home would be there, untouched, by the Grace of God! I told God that I trusted Him and He came through! When the smoke cleared, and every flame doused, there was our home, untouched by the fire. There was not even the smell of smoke inside our house. Truly amazing! Only God could have protected our home.

It was so bad that everyone had to see that it was only God. The way the wind kicked up and was blowing and the bounty of dry tinder to feed that fire, it was truly a miracle. And to have our house completely untouched in any way. I remember being up the street, looking at the black smoke where our home stood, people everywhere, hoping the firemen would soon get this terrible fire under control. All I could say was, "I trust You Lord, You promised." I remember at one point I was reminded of the story in the Bible of Shadrach, Meshech and Abednego. They were thrown into a fiery furnace by the King's command, because they would not bow down and worship a huge golden statue that the King commanded all in his Kingdom to do. They wouldn't do it. Even at the threat of certain death by burning alive!

Well, they were thrown into that furnace, but of course if you've read the story, you know they didn't burn. In fact, a fourth man was seen walking around in that blazing hot furnace with them, and it was Jesus. He never leaves us or forsakes us. When the guards let them out, they did not even smell like smoke. Amazing! Because of that, the King proclaimed that their God was truly the Lord. Praise God! So as I was reminded of that miraculous story, I remember saying to God as I looked at the black smoke, that we were going to come out of this, not even smelling like smoke! And that's exactly what happened! God is so *faithful!* In those desperate moments, He reminds us of His Word that we have stored in our hearts, to strengthen us. We have to stand on His promises no matter what the situation. I'm not saying that it's easy, or that I'm this amazing woman filled with so much faith. It's all God. If we give Him our trust, even when we're hanging on to our faith by a thread sometimes, He gives us what we need to hang on and believe. He'll use a situation like this that seems so horrific and bring glory to His name.

There are so many details of how God and His angels protected our home that day. After the firemen finished, they told us that they were given the word from the Station, that it was hopeless, and to just pack up and leave and let our house go so they could try to secure the rest of the street. But they wouldn't stop. God wouldn't let them. He helped them and strengthened them to do their job, while He did the rest. After they left, newspaper people came to our home with cameras. I told you this was a big fire, and it made the front page of the newspaper. I told them that the only reason that our house was standing was because God saved it. I also told the young woman interviewing me that whatever else she wrote, that that was the most important thing that I wanted her to write. And she did.

I took the news people to the backyard and they were amazed at what they saw. A line of forty foot trees that lined the back of our yard were burned to a crisp, literally. And the bed that they were planted in, was completely black and burned, but the grass line was as green as ever. The fire could not come past our tree line into the yard. I could go on and on with all the amazing details about it. The tree expert in the county came and looked at our property the following week to assess the damage of what he saw. He said that there was no earthly way, given the direction of the wind that day and the dryness of the woods surrounding our home, that our house should be standing. He absolutely agreed with me that it was *Divine Intervention*. A radio reporter came to my door the following morning and interviewed me and another newspaper called me on the phone. Many local newspapers carried the story and all gave glory to God. It was so amazing! I got so many phone calls from people who saw the articles. My God took what could have been a disaster, and protected us and He got all the glory. And when our young son came home that evening, it was just as I said it would be. All of our faith grew so much stronger that day. God is so good and so faithful. All we need to do is to trust Him and to take Him at His Word.

JOE'S CONVERSION

I married my high school sweetheart in 1972. We started dating four years earlier, when I was a sophomore in high school and he was a senior. I was smitten very soon after. He was funny and very handsome and I fell hard! We went to his senior prom together and it was wonderful. But soon after he graduated, he decided college was not for him, so he enlisted in the Marine Corps. He didn't even talk to me about it until the night before he left for Paris Island. We had gone to the movies that night, as we did most weekends. He told me after the movie that he had enlisted in the Marine Corps. I was totally shocked! There had been no previous mention of this at all. I remember asking him when he had to leave, and when he said that he had to go the following morning, I couldn't believe it! I thought he was joking! He couldn't be serious! I thought he was just trying to get a reaction out of me. But unfortunately he wasn't kidding. And when he convinced me that it was true, he did get a reaction, and not a very good one. I was heartbroken! When would I see him again? He said that everything would be ok, but would it? My heart wasn't sure.

Well, my heart survived and he came home two years later after serving in the Vietnam War. He was unharmed, thank God, except for occasional nightmares and a couple of bouts of malaria. I wrote to him everyday. That helped me somehow to keep him close during those long months that seemed like forever. He came home the December of 1970 and we got engaged in February, on Valentine's Day. We got married the following February 12th. My dream came true. God brought my love home and we were married. Inexpressible joy! We went on a wonderful honeymoon and came home a week later to start our storybook life together. Everything would be perfect, right? We were so much in love, we had the rest of our lives together! We had a cute little apartment. Everything I had ever hoped for, except for the children that we hoped would be arriving, very soon.

Well, I think anyone who's been married for a while, finds out sooner or later, that no marriage comes without problems, baggage, in-laws, finances, just to name a few. Things I didn't even think about beforehand. I got my handsome prince and that's all I knew or

JOE'S CONVERSION | 39

cared about! Now let the babies begin! That was my dream. To be a wife and mother. I never went to college. You don't need college to be a wife and mom. I was the oldest daughter of five kids and always helped my mother with the house and all my younger siblings. That was all the college I needed for my dreams!

I've shared all this as a background and a preface to what I really want to share in this chapter. In October of 1975, I invited Jesus Christ to be my Lord and Savior. I grew up Catholic, and believed and knew about God, but did not actually know Him. Unfortunately, before that, Joe and I were Christmas and Easter Catholics, as they say, as far as Church attendance goes. But when I surrendered my heart to Jesus, all that changed. I came to know the God that I always believed in, and for the next forty three years, to this day, I've come to know Him more in every experience of my life, good and bad. Jesus has been there through it all.

I began my new life in Christ at age 23 and was so happy that I just wanted to share this wonderful thing that happened to me with the one person I loved most. My husband. Well, he was not ready for all this Jesus talk and made it clear to me that he wanted me to stop. He told me that he had heard instances where the wife got Jesus and soon after they would get a divorce. I got the hint. So I did stop talking, but began praying! I prayed for the next 27 years! Those years were not easy. To share them all in detail would take a book of its own.

We both had baggage that we brought to the marriage. Joe didn't understand my faith, yet in times of need with his business, he would ask me to pray. He relied on my faith. But if he asked me to pray, it had to be pretty major, because he was very much in control of his life. He was a workaholic and not around much. Though financially he was a great provider, I felt like a single mom a lot of the time. You come to find out that money doesn't make you happy or fill lonely voids. There were times when I didn't know what would happen in our lives, or to our marriage. But I did know that I was God's daughter and that He loved me and my family and that somehow He would make everything right again. How, I didn't know, it seemed impossible sometimes. But nothing is impossible with God!

Joe was a very independent man and he took much pride in "his accomplishments". His company built big roads and bridges, but never put God in the equation. He believed in God, but just did not have time for him. He wasn't even coming to church most Sundays. He always had some work to do at his office or something. He left me to the praying and churchgoing. It was my responsibility to bring the kids to church and teach them about the Lord. But it was also my joy. He actually told me once that He didn't have time to pray. It broke my heart to see him in stressful times, especially business related, and have no one but himself to rely on. I tried to talk to him about God sometimes. He would listen but couldn't understand that he didn't have to do it all alone. There was an inner longing, an emptiness that only God could fill. He tried to fill that need with more money, more things. But no material things ever satisfied. He missed so much with our four children growing up, but he really thought that his most important job was provider. I would try to tell him how much he was missing, and he even agreed, but he couldn't help himself. He was driven. The world and the lure of things had him. He couldn't change. Not on his own anyway. He didn't know the only one who could help him, Jesus.

In the late 90's business was getting very hard. Big problems were arising. Joe thought the only answer was to work harder. He was getting more and more driven! The harder it became and the more problems that arose, the harder he drove himself and his employees. His men were not happy at all to see him drive onto a job site. When he did get home, he would eat, shower, lay on the couch and quietly watch a couple of hours of TV. We didn't speak. I just sat across the room from him...just to be with him. Where had my best friend gone. We could talk for hours in the beginning and laugh. But the cares of the world had chipped away at our marriage and we sat like strangers, just sharing the same oxygen. He kind of cocooned himself from his internal stress and worry of the future. Those couple of hours he just let the TV anesthetize him. Then he'd go to bed. And I kept praying and trusting my Heavenly Father with our lives, our marriage, our future. I prayed so hard for Joe to surrender all his problems to Jesus and accept Him as Lord. I had started praying that Joe would be miserable. Sounds terrible I know, but I prayed that God would protect him, but that he would be miserable on the inside. That he would feel that emptiness in his heart that only God can fill. I prayed that no material wealth or anything else would satisfy him anymore.

By 2002, that prayer would be answered. It had gotten so bad with the business, that Joe finally came to the end of himself. He was mentally and physically exhausted. The man who always had the answers, for us and for everyone else, had finally run out. He had no idea what to do. He had no hope left for the empire he had built. We could possibly lose everything, in his mind. But God had other plans. He came home one night and told me that he didn't know where to go or what to do. He was broken. I never saw him this way before in all the thirty years of our marriage. He said he needed wisdom and asked if I could read the Bible to him. My heart broke for him as we sat down with the Bible. I opened to the book of Proverbs, but I suddenly remembered that a few days earlier in my frustration and concern for my husband, I asked the Lord for a word or a scripture to give to my husband. Ecclesiastes 2, came to mind, and then I forgot about it as quickly as

I thought of it, until that very moment sitting with Joe . I turned to that chapter, from verses 17-22 and read it out loud to him. It was like the words pierced his heart. The Scripture God popped into my head just a few days ago was meant for this very special moment. God is so amazing! This moment in time was precisely planned for the two of us. Joe had me read it over and over again. It was all about a man toiling all his life. Hating the futility of his life because all of his toiling was meaningless. All his work caused him pain and grief and even at night his mind couldn't rest. And one day he would die and all that he worked so hard for all his life would go to someone else. Meaningless, vanity, chasing of the wind.

"So I hated life, for the work which had been done under the sun caused me only great sorrow; because all is futility and chasing after the wind.

So I hated all the fruit (gain) of my labor for which I had labored under the sun, because I must leave it to the man who will succeed me. And who knows whether he will be a wise man or a fool? Yet he will have control over all the fruit of my labor for which I have labored by acting wisely under the sun. This too is vanity (futility, self-conceit).

So I turned aside and let my heart despair over all the fruit of my labor for which I had labored under the sun. For there is a man who has labored with wisdom and knowledge and skill, yet gives his legacy to one who has not labored for it. This too is vanity and a great evil. For what does a man get from all his labor and from the striving and sorrow of his heart with which he labors under the sun?"

— ECCLESIASTES 2:17-22 (AMP)

Joe recognized that this passage of Scripture was describing his life. God is so amazing! After so many years of struggling, depending on his own strength, he finally saw the futility in it and his great need for God. We sat for a while and I listened as he shared with me his brokenness. My heart was filled with love and compassion for my husband, and gratefulness to God. After many precious moments there together, the truth that was revealed to Joe's heart by God was sobering. He needed some time alone and went upstairs to shower. I gave him some time upstairs before I went up to see how he was doing.

As I entered the bathroom, he told me that he was ready to ask Jesus to come into his heart. My heart was racing! All these years of praying and here we were at the moment I had so fervently prayed and believed God for. All Joe's life of struggles. Great highs and low, lows. Always weighing his success as a man on how much his net worth was. Everything bringing him to this moment of truth. His great need for God. I asked him if he wanted me to pray with him, but he wasn't ready for that. He asked me to write a prayer for him and to leave it with his wallet and keys. He'd take it with him in the morning. I went downstairs and sat down and I asked the Holy Spirit to write this prayer through me for Joe. This moment was what I had prayed for, for 27 years. Suddenly it was here! I wept tears of joy as I wrote the simple prayer Holy Spirit gave to me. I also wrote a little note to him, advising him to get alone and shut off his phone as he read. This would be the most important moment of his life. God had waited patiently for him, for many years.

As he left that next morning, I asked him to call me and let me know that he had prayed. He said that he would. I prayed after he left, that God would allow him to experience His Presence in a very special way.

On Joe's job site early that morning, parked under a bridge by himself, he picked up that piece of paper with the prayer and began to read. He said that he struggled beforehand to even pick it up, before he finally did. The enemy of his soul didn't want to let him go. But he did pick it up and barely got through the first few sentences, admitting that he was a sinner in need of a Savior, Jesus, who shed his blood for him, when the Presence of God, filled that truck. He broke down as mercy, forgiveness and love covered him. He would never be the same again!

Over those 27 years, especially in the loneliest,

scariest times, I clung to God. He was all I had and I found out, He was all I ever needed. He was there in the joys, but most importantly, in all the trials of our lives. Whatever I needed to get me through, my loving Heavenly Father always provided and gave me hope to hold on. He had to change me and teach me many things during those years. I was so willing to do whatever He was showing me. Our marriage and our children were worth every tear. It wasn't easy to see some of the things God was showing me about myself that He wanted to help me change, that I had been totally unaware of before. I thought everything was my husband's fault! God lovingly showed me differently and helped me every step of the way as the Holy Spirit revealed things to me. He supplied all that I needed to help me and teach me.

He promises in His Word, never to leave us or forsake us. And true to His word, He never has. He just asks us to trust Him. Jesus said, "Only believe". Joe's conversion was so beautiful. After 30 years, I had a brand new husband, who loves the Lord with all his heart and lives to serve him from that day to this. That was 17 years ago and I'm so thankful! God has blessed us so much to share the rest of our lives loving and serving the Lord together! Joe truly is a *man after God's own heart*. A wonderful husband, father and grandfather. We now pray together for our kids and grandkids and everything else together. I'm not the one in charge of the prayer anymore. We pray together. Praise God! We've watched our kids come to the Lord together and are so blessed to see them all loving Jesus with all their hearts and teaching our grandchildren to love Him too. God has been so faithful!

During the years of waiting, I learned to pray the scriptures. Not only over my husband, but over our children and grandchildren. To *speak those things that be not, as though they were*. I had to learn to let go of offense and learn to forgive, because I was forgiven. That's not so easy most of the time, but if we go to God with trust and a willing heart, He gives us the grace. With God, all things are possible! My husband is a new creation. God makes all things new. We just celebrated 47 years of marriage. We love each other more than ever before. Joe is still funny and handsome, but now he's humble and knows that he needs God every moment of every day. A changed heart is the most beautiful miracle of all! And it's so amazing and beautiful to be able to witness it. I truly am a blessed woman. My God is so faithful and I am eternally grateful!

DON'T CRY OVER SPILLED APPLE JUICE

The experience I'm about to share, taught me something so important about praising God, no matter what's going on in our lives.

At the time I was married about seven years and had two young children, a son about 5 and a daughter 2. At this point in time, my husband and I were not in a good place in our relationship. The saddest part of that might be that my husband was so caught up in his business and the world that he didn't even notice the shambles our relationship had become. We were high school sweethearts and could always talk for hours. Now there was such a distance between us. Maybe an even better way to describe it is that it seemed like a *wall* was between us. We could be sitting across the room from each other watching TV and I would really want to talk to him, but I couldn't think of a single thing to say. I stuffed that reality down deep because if I allowed myself to think about it, it would be unbearable.

I gave my life to Christ four years earlier, but my husband, did not. He also let me know that he wasn't really interested in hearing about that part of my life. That was hard, not being able to share such an important part of my life with my husband. But I complied. He was a workaholic and wasn't home much. More often than not, the kids would be in bed before he got home from work. I was very lonely and truly felt like a single mom. In his mind, he felt like his most important job was to provide for us, which he did very well. But what we really wanted was *him*. This was something that he wouldn't understand until many years later, when he would finally accept Christ for himself.

On a particular Saturday morning, I was very depressed. My husband was away for the weekend, as he was many weekends now. Since he had a stock car built and was now, not only a workaholic during the week, but also the owner of a race car, so his weekends were steeped in that world. I was holding it together with the kids, but continually fighting back tears with thoughts of painful conversations. Like I said, we didn't talk much, but when we did, it was only disagreements about his never being home with us. He would always say that he was working so hard for us, but the race car was a conversation he wouldn't even talk about it. I just had to deal with it. Thank God I had a relationship with Jesus or I most likely would have fallen apart. So that Saturday morning, I was in the kitchen and our son asked for a drink. I went to give him some apple juice. It was only about the second drink I had given him from a brand new half-gallon bottle. As I grabbed the top of the bottle, it broke off at the neck of the bottle. Just like that! It just broke off and crashed to the floor! It didn't hit against anything. It just broke in midair. I never saw anything like it before and haven't seen anything like that happen since. Now there was just shy of a half-gallon of apple juice and shattered glass all over the kitchen floor. Under everything and splattered everywhere! The kids heard the crash and came running to see what had happened. They took one look at the mess, and then at my face, and ran for the hills!

Well, that day was a struggle as it was, so as I took in this overwhelming, horrifying mess, I started crying out to the Lord! Things like, "Oh my God, I can't believe this! I don't need this today! Lord, I'll NEVER get this cleaned up! I don't even know where to start!" That's was just the beginning. Many of the things, I realized afterward, I had been crying out to the Lord about for quite some time now. Things in our lives.

Because I was blessed to be at home with my kids, I was able to watch great Christian ministries on TV and learned a lot over the years since I'd become a Christian. They were a lifeline to me and helped me so much to grow as a Christian. And there was always an 800 number I could call day or night when I desperately needed someone to pray with me. And they always seemed to have the perfect scripture that I needed and always prayed so beautifully and I always hung up feeling more peaceful. In the midst of the apple juice crisis, somehow I remembered that I had learned I was supposed to praise God in every situation. In the midst of my misery, the Holy Spirit reminded me. God is so gracious and loving. So faithful! In those moments I was *definitely not thinking about praising God!* I was miserable and in the process of letting God know about it, in no uncertain terms! But that thought, that memory, broke the noise that I was making. God gave me the grace to hear it and to obey.

Now, when I say obey, I don't mean my tears immediately stopped and I just started praising God wholeheartedly. Oh no! My first inclination was to continue rehearsing my woes to God. After all, God knew very well what I was going through in my marriage. I certainly reminded Him enough. And now this incredible mess, right in the middle of me feeling sorry for myself. This was more than I could handle. At least without my loving Father it would have been! The Holy Spirit whispered the thought for me to praise, and though I struggled with it at first, He gave me the grace to try. Very begrudgingly at first, I might add. I reached for a roll of paper towel and got a paper bag and got on my knees to try to clean up this daunting mess! Taking care not to kneel on broken glass, I began praising God, begrudgingly...as I said, one wipe at a time. As I continued wiping and praising, the wiping, and much more importantly the praising, got much easier. It actually went from agony and lip service as I thanked God with every handful of glass and apple juice, to effortless praise to my God, who loved me so much and saw me on that sticky floor. He saw the pain in my heart and my attempt to praise Him through it, and He came down and helped me Himself. I'm not saying that I saw Him next to me on the floor, but He was there with me.

The Bible says that He inhabits the praises of His people. I had given Him something to inhabit, no matter how weak I started out. I don't know how long it took, but all of a sudden I looked around me and the floor and everything else was clean! It was amazing! Something I thought was so impossible was now done. All things are possible with God. And the instant I stood and looked around me at this clean floor, I heard the Lord speak to me. Not audibly, but His voice was so clear inside of me. He said, "You see Stephanie. You thought you'd never clean that mess up, but we cleaned it up together. And just like I helped you clean this mess up, I'm going to help you clean the mess in your life." Well, as you can imagine, I was crying and praising God all over again! With those words, God breathed hope back into my heart. Hope for our marriage and our future. I knew God loved me and my husband and our children more than I did, and that nothing was impossible, if I would only believe. I held onto His promise, until it came to pass.

Well, God did help me clean up the mess my husband and I were in. It wasn't overnight. Far from it! It was a long process. God taught me so much and changed me so much in that process. And it wasn't easy and there were still many more tears to be shed all along the way. But I had His promise to cling to, and God is a Promise Keeper. He had to teach me so much about myself that I wasn't even aware of. Things I didn't necessarily want to see. I always thought the whole problem was my husband, but there's two in any relationship. I was the Christian in the equation that had a willing heart, and would allow Him to work with and in me. He always gave me what I needed to hold on.

Sometimes, we are so loud when things in our lives are in a turmoil, that we can't hear that still, small voice of the Holy Spirit inside of us. If we will just quiet ourselves and praise Him, no matter how hard it is, even if it is not wholehearted at first...He will meet us there, because He truly inhibits our praise. He is so patient and loving, and He sees our pain and understands how hard it is to praise Him in the worst of times. But that worship is so precious to Him. It is so easy to praise Him when everything is going well in our lives, but *oh the praise that costs us something.* In the middle of the greatest storms in our lives, to praise Him. How much more valuable is that worship to Him. To trust Him when you can't see through the storm and you just thank Him for being there with you. If Jesus is in the boat with you, there is no storm that can take you under! When He's all you have, that's great, because He's all you need. He'll bring us to the other side better, and stronger if we just trust Him. He'll never leave us or forsake us. *He promised*.

My husband and I have been married now for 47 years. Joe got saved 17 years ago, many years after that apple juice incident. We've been praising God together now for all the many blessings in our lives. Our God is faithful and we are so very grateful!

MY BRACELET

This is a story about how God taught me about tithing and giving, especially when it's hard. Many years ago my husband asked me to pray for his contracting company. We needed work badly. Before he turned his life over to the Lord, he left all the praying up to me. So, of course, I prayed. One morning I was watching a favorite Christian program of mine. It was during their telethon week that they had once a year. This Christian organization was a huge source of strength and faith for me. Especially as a young Christian, the daily testimonies blessed me and strengthened my faith. Every time I had a need, I could, and did call their 24-hour prayer line and was blessed and comforted by the time I got off the phone. For the last almost 40 years, until now, this ministry holds a very special place in my heart.

So on this particular morning of the telethon, I wanted so much to give something to the ministry that was there for me anytime I needed them. I didn't know how I could though because, at that early stage of our married life, I didn't even have a checkbook. So I prayed and asked God what I could give. He gave me a very unexpected and unsettling answer. You see, my husband had given me a beautiful antique opal bracelet as a gift on our wedding day. You guessed it! That's what God told me to give. Of course at first I thought "That can't be God, asking for my wedding gift." I prayed for a week in the hopes that I was mistaken and would hear something else from the Lord. But no, all I heard was my bracelet. I came to understand that my true Bridegroom, Jesus, was asking for my wedding gift. Something of sacrifice and meaning.

Although the bracelet was not overly expensive in dollar value, it was precious to me. So, I set my heart to give my bracelet. And when I finally did that, I became aware of a Christian women's meeting, where they had special guest speakers. The guest speaker this time would be someone that was the cohost of the very ministry that I was giving my bracelet too. Some coincidence. And it was being held only about 40 minutes from my home. I had planned to mail my bracelet, but now I could just bring my bracelet to the meeting and place it in the speaker's hands, to deliver to the ministry for me. I could then ask him to pray with me for the great financial need we had! I was excited. But when I woke up the morning of the meeting, I felt terrible. I was tempted not to go, but I pushed through. I knew I had to go. It was a wonderful meeting. He shared his amazing testimony and afterwards invited anyone who needed prayer to come up front. I brought my bracelet up and told him of our great financial need and that I was planting my bracelet, my wedding gift, into the hands of my true Husband, in faith. I held my bracelet in my hands and he clasped his huge hands around mine, and prayed.

Within two weeks, my husband got the biggest contract for work that he'd ever gotten before. It was over a million dollar job! That was a major multiplication of the small, but precious gift that I had planted for the work of the Lord. It wasn't small to the Lord though. Even in comparison to what He gave back to us, He saw the sacrifice and knew it had been hard for me at first. As a matter of fact, I didn't tell my husband what I did for quite a while. When I finally did, he was thankful. That was my very first experience in giving that way. I had such a desire to give to a ministry that blessed and encouraged me so much, but thought I had nothing to give, until I asked the Lord. Even though I hesitated and it took me a week of praying, I knew I had heard His voice and wanted to obey. What He asked for was precious to me, but what He gave back was priceless. An increased trust and faith in Him and His faithfulness. If we will just trust Him in the most difficult times, He will always bring us through to the other side stronger and knowing our wonderful Savior and His great love for us more intimately.

I entrusted my gift into His hands and He multiplied it back many times over, financially, but even more importantly, causing my faith and love to multiply. All the while, He was at work in my husband as well. If God asks you to do something difficult, know that the dividends of our obedience are far greater than anything we could ever hope for or imagine. He truly is the *exceedingly, abundant God*. I love Him so much.

WATCH THAT TRUCK

*M*any years ago, my husband, who wouldn't come to know Jesus for many years yet, had a very close call on his job site that helped him to begin to believe in miracles. He was on his construction site and he was trying to figure out what was wrong with his dump truck. Actually this wasn't the first miracle he experienced that involved his trucks. In this instance, he realized that the hydraulic line was leaking.

Apparently, that's not a good thing, so he raised the body of the truck so that he could climb under and take a closer look. Climbing under truck bodies is not advisable, especially on that particular day with that particular truck. As Joe was bent over trying to find the leak, the body of the truck was slowly coming down without him knowing it. Whatever mechanism holds that truck body up, was slowly disengaging without Joe realizing that the truck body was getting closer and closer to crushing him. Job sites are very noisy, which could explain why on earth he didn't even hear something was wrong. Suddenly someone grabbed Joe by the shoulder and yanked him out from under there, just a second before that truck body slammed down all the way. Joe would have been crushed if this person hadn't noticed his plight and literally pulled him out just in time and saved his life! He instantly whirled around to see who his rescuer was to thank him for saving his life. To his great shock, *there was no one there*. He looked in every direction. No one!

There is a beautiful Psalm in the bible that I had found and put to memory and as a habit prayed it over my family most every day and still do over 40 years later. Psalm 91:9-11 says, *"If you make the Most High your dwelling, even the Lord, Who is my refuge, then no harm will befall you, no disaster will come near your tent. For He will command His angels, concerning you to guard you in all your ways."* The entire Psalm is full of glorious promises of protection. I know my husband was saved that day by an angel. God is so faithful to His word. I believe His word and speak it every day, over our family and every situation in our lives. We take Him at His Word and He is faithful to bring it to pass.

I could have lost my husband that day. Instead God miraculously saved him and he increased our trust and faith once again. It took Joe many years before he gave his life to Jesus, but he never doubted that he was saved by God that day. Over the next couple of decades, God would continue to intervene in Joe's life. In all of our lives. He never gives up on us. And in May of 2002, Joe was gloriously converted. He's been loving and serving God now for many years. God is so faithful! Never give up on your loved ones! Keep praying and believing for them for God hears your prayers and is faithful!

MICHELLE'S BACK

*M*any years ago when my youngest daughter, who is now almost 38, was a teenager in high school, she tried out for the track team. She started going to the practices after school and before too long, she started complaining about pain in her lower back that radiated all the way down her right leg into her foot. She started popping ibuprofen a few times a day for the pain. All her friends knew where they could get the ibuprofen when they needed it. At first we thought that she had just pulled something and that it would just work its way out with time.

Of course, when I would see her in pain, I would pray for her, believing in my heart that God would heal her. We took her to a specialist in Philadelphia, as she seemed to get no relief. The doctor took x rays and explained to us that Michelle had a weakness in her lower spine. It never bothered her until she started running track. Apparently, this new strenuous physical activity put a great strain in this area of her spine, causing this pressure and pain. He said that short of surgery, which she was too young for, she would have to do a regimen of stretches for her back every day for the rest of her life to help manage the pain. Twice a day for two months, and then once a day for the rest of her life. And of course, no more track.

She resolved to do her stretches and she did them religiously for the two months and the pain did go away, so she stopped. She thought that she was fine, but soon the pain returned. She became angry and bitter and began taking the ibuprofen again. Whenever she came home from school in pain, sometimes in tears, I would pray with her. She expressed to me one day her fear of having children someday, because she knew it wasn't wise to take medication while pregnant. I thought my heart would break, seeing my daughter in pain all the time, and hearing her concerns for the future. I would try to encourage her to believe for her healing. We prayed so many times, but the pain just persisted. I'll never forget the day she came home in tears in so much pain and I offered to pray with her as usual. It broke my heart when her response to me was, "No thanks Mom, been there, done that".

She gave up all hope that God would heal her. She

thought she was destined to a life of pain, filled with fear for her future. I never gave up hope. I continued praying.

During these few years, I had been watching a famous faith healer. God used him powerfully, but sometimes when Holy Spirit moved on people in his audience, it was very new to me. Even a little startling. I had never seen this side of God. We need to be open to the many different ways that God's presence manifests. Anyway, I was determined to listen to this man of God teach, so I could understand better what he believed. Everything he said rang true in my heart, so I continued watching and became much more comfortable with what God was doing during his services. Sometimes Michelle would walk in the room when I was watching, right in the middle of the healing service, where he would speak one word and the whole audience would fall back under the power of God. I remember one particular morning she came in and rolled her eyes and retorted, "Mom, really, you believe this stuff? Come on, seriously?" I would reply that I did, and she would look at me, incredulously and walk away.

My heart hurt that my daughter's precious faith was being so severely tested and she had pretty much given up on God healing her. I kept watching and praying and believing enough for the both of us. Soon after that incident, I was watching and they announced that this ministry would be coming to our area very soon. The church where I attended prayer meetings rented a bus so that the people from our group could attend. I decided to go and bring my kids. Many others signed up. We knew crowds would be coming from everywhere and it would be an all day affair, and into the night. My daughter put up a big stink because she had just graduated right before the service, and it would be on a Friday and she didn't want to give up any Friday nights with her friends before leaving for College. I gave her no choice, and she was on that bus! It was an amazing service and my family and I were believing in our hearts for Michelle's healing. My oldest daughter Danielle, told her sister she would be healed that night. Michelle shrugged it off. She later told me that she was afraid to believe that it could happen. She didn't want her hopes to be dashed again! Beautiful worship filled that huge arena as thousands of people stood together singing and worshipping God. It was amazing! Then the minister, who was leading us in the worship, said to us, "Jesus is here, just ask Him for what you need." In that moment my daughter-in-law, who was sitting behind Michelle, was moved to put her hand on the base of Michelle's back.

Michelle's back was completely healed that night. The minister, or a healing team, didn't have to even lay hands on her, but the power of our God touched her right where she stood. She didn't say a word to us and we didn't ask. She didn't take any ibuprofen that night to see if it could possibly be true. Dare she hope that her pain would not return? God had heard the cry of her heart for healing, that was buried beneath the emotional pain caused by years of disappointment. She woke up the next morning, pain free!

She didn't take the meds all that next week and tested her back out every way she knew, doing all the things that would normally cause her great pain. One thing in particular was when she would squat down, her hip would lock and she wouldn't be able to get up without help from someone and pain. She decided to clean her room that week because she knew that would require a lot of squatting. To her surprise and great joy, she was able to get right up from that position without any pain! She had been keeping all this to herself all week, but she finally, truly believed she was healed, and felt she could share this wonderful miracle with her family! We all rejoiced and praised God for His good-ness. God is so good and so faithful, and His timing is always perfect.

You may wonder why God didn't heal her sooner? Why did she have to suffer for four years, waiting for her healing and having her faith challenged so much? Only God really knows, but as I look back at the couple of years before her healing, Michelle was starting to do some of those things that no parents want their kids to be involved in. Smoking, drinking, making some very wrong choices that definitely kept me on my knees. Soon she would be off to another state to start college. There would be much more temptation to do more of the same things and maybe worse, feeling the freedom of being away and on her own. I believe God's timing was perfect! He knows Michelle inside and out! He created her! He knew exactly what she was doing, and what she'd be facing!

She gave her heart to Jesus as a little girl, but at this point in her life, she was hanging out with the wrong kids and certainly not living out her faith. God miraculously healed her at this point in her life, when she needed His touch the most. Her faith, that got buried by disappointment and pain, got miraculously resurrected! God had completely healed her! He had shown up *big time!* Perhaps if she had been healed right away, without much suffering, it wouldn't have made such an impact. It wouldn't have meant so much and might have been soon forgotten. God is so smart! He does all things well and His ways are perfect! In this perfect timing of her healing, she experienced a life changing faith. Now, I am in no way saying that God withheld her healing in order that *much pain would cause her to appreciate her healing more.* I don't believe that for a second. God is good. As a matter of fact, if Michelle had continued with her exercises from the start, she wouldn't have suffered that pain. She made the choice, not only to quit her stretches, but most importantly to quit believing that God would heal her. So that when she was healed in an atmosphere of great faith, very little of which was hers, her heart opened up and her faith was restored and her life took a very different turn. I'm not saying that she became the perfect little Christian. She struggled at times, like we all do and will until we are with Jesus. But she knew what He did and she knew He would always be there through every struggle this life would try to throw at her. That is the glorious grace of our God.

There is so much to her testimony, between then and now, just under 20 years ago. Now she is 37 and happily married to a wonderful young man who she met at church. Michelle and her husband are both in ministry now for many years and are committed to serving the Lord and the Body of Christ with all their hearts. They have two beautiful daughters and a beautiful little son, who are growing up to know and love Jesus. What more could grandparents ask for? God is so faithful! *He makes all things work together for our good, because we love Him and are called according to His purpose. (Romans 8:28)*

Many times we face really hard things we don't understand. Our prayers seem to be unanswered in the midst of the storms of our lives. Believe me, I've been there, but I know that if we just keep trusting God, no matter how impossible it may seem, He is with us and He is faithful. There is nothing impossible for God!

Where can we go if we give up on our loving God? Our only help, our strength, our comfort, our joy...and the list goes on! In my almost 44 years of history with God, He has never failed me or my family and He never will. He's so faithful and I'm eternally grateful!

YOU CAN'T OUTGIVE GOD

*M*any, many years ago, I believe it was in the eighties, my husband had a very big problem in his contracting company. Actually, it was more in the category of *crisis,* because if things didn't end up well, we could have lost everything! Our business and our home. In short, we needed a miracle! Big time! Well, I was a Christian and believed in miracles. However, my husband was not. He did not give his life to Christ until 2002, which was many years later, so whenever there were business problems of any kind or size, he asked me to pray. And of course, I did.

As the days and weeks progressed, things seemed to get more and more bleak and seemingly impossible to overcome. Those are the times God can really show off big time. My husband would keep telling me how bad it was and that we could lose everything and he got more and more stressed out, because in the natural, that's what it looked like. But because I was a Christian, I knew that I was God's daughter and that He loved us and had an answer no matter how bad it looked, and that we wouldn't lose anything that God had given us. I would tell my husband that and he hoped that what I said was true. My voice was the only positive voice he heard. My heart hurt for him as I watched him struggle, without that deep knowing that God loved him and could really get him out of his mess. God gives us a peace in the midst of the storm. Without knowing God, he couldn't experience that amazing peace that passes all understanding. I continued to pray and believe God, and tried to encourage my husband as much as I could. I prayed for Joe continually as well.

One day, when I was alone with God, praying, I felt God asking me to tell Joe that he should give ten percent of his paycheck every week. I was taken aback by what I felt God was asking of me and frankly uneasy at the thought of going to my husband with this. I couldn't imagine what my husband would say to me, knowing what he was going through. I prayed for a week, asking God to remove this thought if it truly wasn't Him, but if it truly was Him, to please give me the courage to tell my husband. Well, after a week of praying, I realized it truly was God and I prayed for the right moment to speak. I was a little apprehensive to say the least. That moment came and we sat together and I told him what I believed the Lord had asked me to tell him. Almost without hesitation, he said, 'ok'.

There was no argument or long pause, or incredulous look as he told me I was crazy for even suggesting such a thing at a time like this. No! Nothing that I had imagined that he might say. I didn't have to reason with him, pull out a Scripture on tithing, or anything! Amazing! Out of his sheer desperation for an answer, and hoping against hope that this was truly God, he just said, ok! God is so amazing! Well, Joe gave me a tenth of his paycheck week after week, without fail. Things didn't get better right away. As a matter of fact they got worse before they got better, but Joe was faithful to give every week, no matter what things looked like.

Sometimes I felt bad taking it from him, but only for a brief moment, because it was God and He is faithful. We have certainly learned over the years that you can't out give God. He blessed our faithfulness to what He asked of us, and He did rescue us in an amazing way. When it was all over, our business and home were intact, and not only that, but God blessed us abundantly! We ended up in better shape financially at the end of the crisis than before it began. It truly was a miracle! God taught us both about giving through that crisis. Even though it might seem like the craziest thing in the world to do. You're losing money every day, and God asks you to give from your need. The tendency in the world is, when things get tight, hold onto what you have for dear life and don't let go!

But with God, it's the opposite. If we trust Him, and put what little we have in His hands, He multiplies it back to us. The Bible says "Give and it shall be given unto you. Pressed down, shaken together and running over. I had learned it and believed it as a Christian, but it had never been put to the test like that. And my husband was just hoping beyond hope that it was true. In his desperate situation, he was open to whatever I said because he knew I had a relationship with God and prayed.

Almost 20 years later, Joe gave his life to Christ. He has been a giver ever since then. There have been highs and lows in our finances over the years, but we've remained faithful givers and God has always been true to His Word. He has always supplied our needs according to His riches in Glory, by Christ Jesus. He has always taken care of and blessed Joe and I and our kids and grandkids. He is so faithful! His Word cannot fail, if we'll only trust Him. He has promised to always take care of us, to never leave us or forsake us and He never has and never will. We just need to trust Him and take Him at His Word. His Word stands forever. God is so good and my family and I are forever grateful!

THAT DARN KNEE

*I*t was many years ago now, probably 40. My younger sister, who is 16 years younger than me, was about 10 at the time. She used to spend a lot of time at our house during the summers. I was married with children at the time of the incident I'm about to describe. We have a pool and she loved spending time with the kids. She'd even bring her best friend sometimes and they would spend days enjoying fun in the sun together.

Well, my sister had a bump under her knee. It must have been hereditary because our father had the same bump. It wasn't something that you would really notice, unless it was pointed out, but if she bumped into something and hit that bump, she saw stars! It didn't bother her at all, unless she bumped it.

One particular week, while she was staying at our

house in the summer, was a banner week for her bumping that knee. All week long I remember Chris yelping in pain. I felt so bad for my cute little sister, but I couldn't believe it! How could you possibly bump the same knee so many times?! Seriously!! Me, being a Christian who believed in healing, took to the end of the week and I don't know how many yelps of pain, before I finally said, "Let's ask God to heal your knee!" Well, I guess better late than never! I wasn't sure that she would want to but she readily agreed to the prayer.

I had a prayer cloth in my bible that came from a wonderful ministry that I followed. The idea was that the cloth would be a point of contact for our faith, as I placed it on her knee and asked Jesus to heal her. Most importantly, I asked her if she believed that Jesus could heal her and she, without hesitation, said she did believe. That's all Jesus asks us to do. Believe. So, I prayed for her healing, in the name of Jesus. After I finished praying, she decided to test it out, so with her fist, she began banging on her knee. After the first couple of punches, she looked up at me with astonishment! No pain! She kept punching, to make sure! Still no pain! She was healed! We laughed and hugged with tears of joy and praised Jesus for His goodness. Well, that was 40 years ago and it hasn't bothered her since.

Jesus spoke about us having the faith of a child and about believing that when we pray about anything, we should believe that what we're praying for is already done. Coming to our Lord, believing that His Word is true, and is for us today. That we can really expect to receive the miracles that we need. My little sister learned that morning at an early age, as my faith was deepened, that God really hears and answers our heart's cries. I'm so grateful. And so was little Sis!

GOD GAVE HER A SONG

This story began about 24 years ago, when our youngest son, Michael, was in the first grade. I became one of his 'class moms'. I soon hit it off with the other 'class mom', who to this day is my best friend. We started spending time together and really began to get to know one another. She shared with me about her three year old daughter, Brianna, who had been diagnosed with severe asthma at twenty months of age. It was a very difficult and heart rending situation. She was on a nebulizer machine three times a day, just for maintenance, unless she got sick. If she had an infection of any kind that caused her temperature to rise to 101 or more, that complicated matters greatly. She would have to go on the machine every two hours and take steroids if her breathing got bad. She could go into febrile seizures if not taken care of swiftly and properly. Besides needing these medications to breathe and maintenance on a machine, she couldn't be around certain very strong smells, like fresh paint or incense. These things would throw her into a convulsion and she would have to be rushed to the Emergency Room. Convulsions caused her eyes to roll back and her mouth to foam. She couldn't be outside playing in the cold winter, because her chest would tighten up. And to top it all off, she was allergic to bee stings as well. Our hearts and our prayers went out to this precious little girl, who suffered so much, even with all the loving care of her family. Terry would call me exhausted from worry and so many trips to the E.R., while also working a part time job. I would pray with my friend and try to encourage her that God would heal her beautiful child. I believed He would, but her faith was being sorely tested and failing.

At some time during the next year or so, I led Terry to accept Jesus Christ as her Lord and Savior. We continued to pray and believe for Bri's healing. Though Terry still struggled greatly with her faith as she continued to see no change. Her husband also became a Christian shortly after Terry did, which was a blessing, because even though it was so difficult , they had a trust in God that they didn't have before.

There is nothing more difficult than to see your child suffer. You feel so helpless. Any one of us would gladly take our children's pain for them. Sometimes we feel so alone in our pain, but we are never alone if we have Jesus. He is our Help, our Comfort, our Healer. *He will never leave or forsake us. (Hebrews 13:5)* Even if you are hanging on by a thread, keep holding on to your end, because Jesus is holding His end. He will never let go.

A couple more years went by, with more trips to the E.R., more medication, more prayer, but still no change in Brianna's physical condition. By this time, Bri was about seven and we heard that an extremely famous Christian minister, who had a very powerful healing ministry, was coming to a stadium not far from our town. Well, we of course made plans to bring Bri, hoping beyond hope that Jesus would heal this sweet child. Terry was really finding it hard to believe anything would happen after all those years, but we encouraged her. God had brought this Man of God so close and we couldn't *not go.* I truly believed God was going to do many great things at this meeting, including healing Bri. Well, that night after the beautiful worship, the minister encouraged us to just reach out and ask the Lord for what we needed. We all prayed, including little Bri. Terry still struggled to believe, but God honors our faith, even when it seems so small to us. We all put our faith together, including little Bri and we prayed. We enjoyed the rest of the service and then went home. Before Tommy and Terry put Brianna to bed, at the time when they would normally be giving her medication, Bri burst out with, 'I don't want my medicine, I'm healed!' She told her parents that during the prayer, she felt and heard music in her lungs! So amazing! Music in her lungs! Now this was a huge step of faith for them to just stop the meds, cold turkey, because under normal circumstances this could be very dangerous! You have to be weaned off these medications! That is, of course, unless the Lord supernaturally heals you! Normal gets thrown out the window when God shows up!

As you might have guessed by now, they decided to completely trust God, although it was very scary. Sometimes stepping out in faith can be very scary, but God is so faithful! And of course, Bri was completely healed and has never taken that medication again. Only one time that winter was Terry tempted to give her something. Bri was outside, playing in the cold with her friends. This was something she could never do before God healed her. Her chest started to hurt and she ran in to her mom, to tell her. Terry called me to ask my advice on what to do. I could hear in her voice that she was struggling with her faith. Her voice was trembling as she tried to hold back her tears. I felt an anger rise up in me! The enemy of our soul was trying to scare Terry into giving her medication! He wanted to steal her healing with his scare tactics! I thank God for the grace He gave me in that moment to tell Terry that the devil is a liar and that Brianna was completely healed and needed no medication. I'll never forget her voice as she very weakly responded, 'ok'. She believed me, but more importantly, she believed God, and Bri has never had a problem since. God even healed her of her allergy to bee stings, that could potentially be very dangerous if not treated immediately with an EpiPen. God is so amazing. He is the same yesterday, today and forever! He is forever our *healer*.

Bri is 24 years old now and she sings for a living and is one of the worship leaders in our church. God has gifted her with a beautiful voice and we all know you need plenty of lung power for that. The enemy tried to steal her breath, but God healed her. She knew it because she heard and felt music in her lungs! How amazing and beautiful! And the breath in her lungs is being used to worship and glorify the God who loves and healed her. I watch and listen to her worship at church, and weep at the goodness and faithfulness of our God. God touched her lungs, changed her life dramatically and filled her with a faith and a love for God that will carry her through her life. She is a beautiful young woman with an amazing testimony of God's love and faithfulness. Praise His holy name.

MY HEALER

$\mathcal{I}$ am about to share what God did for me just about two months ago. I was diagnosed in September with a very small lump in my breast. I went for all the tests, a 3D mammogram, biopsy, MRI. From the first mammogram when the doctor detected the abnormality, I trusted and believed that it would be benign. My family was believing with me. However, the tests came back positive and I was told it would have to be removed and that surrounding tissue and some lymph nodes would also be removed for testing at the time of the surgery. Needless to say, it was not the news we were hoping for, but I trusted in the Lord who has always been faithful and I expressed this belief to the nurse on the phone. When I hung up, I slid to my knees, and tearfully told the Lord that I trusted Him and that I knew I was healed, because His

Word promised me, even if He chose to use the surgeon to manifest His healing in my body. My family and I continued to confess and trust in God's Word with me for my complete healing.

In preparation for the surgery, I added healing scriptures to my morning quiet time with the Lord. I treasure this time with the Lord, where I just sit with Him and worship Him and thank Him for His goodness. I pray and read the Bible and pour out my heart to Him. It's there I'm filled with His peace and I experience His presence in such a special and intimate way. One of the scriptures I continually confessed, and still do, over me and my family is Isaiah 53:4-5. *"Surely He has borne our sicknesses and carried our disease, yet we did esteem Him stricken, smitten of God and afflicted. But He was pierced for our transgressions. He was crushed for our iniquities, the punishment that brought us peace was upon Him, and by His wounds we are healed."*

Over and over I would repeat these verses, especially at night when it was quiet and I was in bed trying to sleep and the enemy of my soul would try to bring fear. I would fight back with the weapon my Lord has given me. *His glorious Word!* I would ask Holy Spirit to protect my mind. I would silently sing in my mind a song of God's faithfulness. Soon, sleep would come.

Another Scripture I love to repeat when thoughts come that try to contradict the Word of God for my life is Isaiah 41:10. *"So do not fear, for I am with you; do not be dismayed, for I am your God. I will strengthen you and help you. I will uphold you with My righteous right hand".* Oh how this Scripture has comforted me ever since I first discovered it! The Word of God has comforted, strengthened and kept me for the last 43 years, since I gave my heart to Jesus all those years ago. I have believed it and confessed it over myself and my loved ones through every difficult and even heartbreaking time in our lives.

God stands by His Word! Hebrews 4:12 *"For the Word of God is living and active. Sharper than any double edged sword; it penetrates even to dividing soul and spirit, joints and marrow. It judges the thoughts and attitudes of the heart."* There is nothing more powerful than God's Word. God spoke and the world came into being. Jesus is the Word that became flesh. John 1:14, *"The Word became flesh and made His dwelling among us. We have seen His glory, the glory of the One, Who came from the Father, full of grace and truth."*

I am so grateful to God for His Words of truth, life, healing, faithfulness and so much more! It has never failed me and never will. His character, love and promises are all right there in the Word of God, just waiting for us to meditate on and hide them in our hearts. Once they have been hidden there, as we spend time in the secret place with God, we can draw on them and be comforted and strengthened by them in the trials of this life. And let's face it, we all experience those times of trial, but when we have Jesus, we have everything we need to get through. And in those difficult times, if we continue to cling to Him, we come to experience Him in a way we never would if our lives were problem free. He is completely faithful and we can trust Him with everything. Our hearts, our families, our feelings, all of our hurts and concerns. Our whole lives. He is here and cares about it all. No matter how big or small, we just bring it to Him with an open heart. He knows it all anyway. There's just something so freeing about getting on our knees, before His throne of Grace, and bringing everything. Your tears. Your fears. Holding nothing back from the One who created you and knows everything about you. The good, the bad, everything, and yet He sees us as righteous, perfect, holy. He is waiting with open arms, with a limitless, everlasting love, because of what Jesus did for us on the Cross.

I've gone to the Lord, full of anxiety because the enemy was bringing an old memory that I just couldn't shake until I got on my knees and gave it to the Lord and cried in His arms. I walked out of that room at peace and free. You see the enemy is the accuser. He just wants to remind us of our past sins and mistakes. He wants us to feel condemned and steal our peace. But once we've made Jesus our Lord, everything from the past is covered with the blood of Jesus. Forgiven and forgotten by our beautiful Savior. Romans 8:1,

"There is now no condemnation to them which are in Christ Jesus, who walk not after the flesh, but after the Spirit". So the enemy can try his hardest to condemn us, but we've been bought with a precious price. The precious Blood of Jesus, And all we have to do is run to Him! We are victorious in Christ! Romans 8:37 *"No, in all these things we are more than conquerors through Him, Who loved us."* The enemy has no power over us! It was destroyed on the Cross! Hallelujah!

I can never thank my Lord enough for all He has done for me and my family... starting with *the cross*. I am so grateful! So, getting back to my healing testimony. For the couple of weeks I had between the diagnosis and the surgery, I fought off the enemy's attacks with the Word of God and worshipping Him and thanking Him for my complete healing. My family did the same. During the consultation with the surgeon, where she explained what she would do, I was at peace and was able to share my faith and trust in God...*my Healer.* My doctor even remarked on the difference between me and most of her patients, in that she noticed that I was calm and peaceful and full of confidence in God. Only with Jesus was I able to be at peace and a witness of God's goodness in that circumstance, instead of scared and anything but peaceful! Jesus promises us peace in the midst of our storms. Phil. 4:7 *"And the peace of God which surpasses all understanding, will guard your hearts and minds through Christ."* Praise

God! How often over the last 43 years have I experienced that peace?! A peace you can get nowhere else but from God. Our personal world can be out of control with no answer in sight, but if we trust in God and in His glorious Word, we can experience His peace and rest through it all.

Well, the surgery went perfectly. All lymph nodes and surrounding tissue perfect, and my surgeon was extremely happy to tell me the good news that I knew I would hear. My God is faithful. Of course, my surgeon, being a student of medicine and science, advised me to see an oncologist, who she said would probably put me on radiation for one month...just as a precautionary measure, of course. Why... just in case God didn't do a good enough job on the cross? Just in case He missed something? No way would I even consider it. I'm completely healed! Jesus accomplished it on the cross and used an excellent surgeon who was guided by His hand to bring about the manifestation of His healing in my body. Praise His Holy Name! He removed all that didn't belong in my body and allowed me to share my faith with every nurse that attended me, as well as my surgeon. I pray God waters the seeds of faith I sowed into those lovely people I encountered there and that God used to minister to me. I thank God for His amazing grace that brought me through again victoriously! Hallelujah! God is so faithful!

One of the most important things I've learned over

the last 43 years with the Lord is to spend quality time with Him. Worshipping Him, reading and meditating on His Word. Hiding it in my heart. Memorizing scriptures that speak to my everyday needs and confessing them over myself, my loved ones and over every situation in our lives, every day. His Word has comforted me, strengthened me, taught me, changed me. It cannot fail. (Isaiah 55:11) *"So is my Word that goes out from my mouth; it will not return to me empty, but will accomplish what I desire and achieve the purpose for which I sent it."* All we have to do is believe it and keep confessing it in faith! No matter how long it takes, until our victory has manifested. And it will! And very important, through it all, praise Him!

Many times through tears, but thank Him for His faithfulness, goodness and love. We could never run out of things to praise God for! Just waking up in the morning is a gift! No matter how we are feeling, if we just give Him that precious, sacrificial praise, He will lift us up by His precious Holy Spirit and we will experience peace. Praising Him throughout all eternity will still not be enough for all of His goodness and faithfulness to me and my family. The greatest gift of all, of course, being *eternal life*. The precious blood of Jesus that was shed for us all. All we have to do is *receive it.* He took our sins, our punishment and disease and destroyed it on the cross. And when we believe, He gives us His righteousness and perfect standing before our Holy God. Eternal life, forever with Him, and the glorious gift of His Holy Spirit, who will never leave us or forsake us. The very Spirit that raised Christ from the dead makes His home in us. Romans 11. And He even has given us the faith to believe! It is all His glorious Grace! How can I ever thank my Lord enough for all He is and all He has done for me and my family. It's impossible, but I'll never stop! We are forever grateful!

If you haven't yet made a decision for Christ, I encourage you to make the most important decision of your life. He's waiting with open arms and an ever-lasting love for you.

"May the God of hope fill you with all joy and peace as you trust in Him, so that you may overflow with hope by the power of the Holy Spirit."

— ROMANS 15:13

"But I trust in Your unfailing love. My heart rejoices in Your Salvation. I will sing to the Lord, for He has been good to me."

— PSALM 13:5-6 NIV

INVITATION TO SALVATION

Maybe you have never experienced a relationship with God like the one I've written about in this book. I can't imagine what my life would have been like, if not for my wonderful Savior. He truly is Forever Faithful! He's only a prayer away. He loves you with an everlasting love and if you'll say this simple prayer with all your heart, He'll be your Forever Faithful God too:

Dear Heavenly Father, I want this relationship that Jesus died to give me. I believe that Jesus lived and that He died for me on the Cross and that He rose again and lives forevermore. I invite You, Jesus, to come and live in my heart. Forgive my sins and take my life and help me to live for You. Thank You for loving me and giving Your life for me so that I may have new life in You. In Jesus name, Amen.

It's as simple as that. If you prayed that prayer and meant it with all your heart, Jesus has made His home in you. Get ready for an adventure with the One who loves you with an everlasting, unconditional love. He will never leave you or forsake you. Find a great church where you feel at home, and get to know God in His Word, which never fails. You'll find that He truly is *Forever Faithful.*

AFTERWORD

I'm so thankful for all the many wonderful things that God has done for me and my family. Those contained in these pages, and those that are not. But what I'm most thankful for is that God saved us all. That is the greatest Miracle of all! Changed hearts and changed lives!

During those twenty seven years of waiting for my husband to give his life to Jesus Christ, there were wonderful years as well. We had rough times as I'm sure most marriages do, but God got us through them all , and taught us and changed us so much. Our love for God and each other grew stronger with each victory. Joe loved us and did his best for us in his own strength, until he had no strength left and gave it all to Jesus. Jesus was waiting all along with open arms. Just like He is for all of us. His conversion was so beautiful to witness. I cried many tears of joy. His love and gratitude to Jesus was so evident and beautiful to witness. Now I had a prayer partner and together we've prayed and stood on God's Word for each other, our kids and grandkids and whatever challenges come our way. And together, for the last almost eighteen years, we've watched our kids give their lives to Jesus, and with their spouses, they are loving and serving Jesus with all their hearts and teaching our grandkids to do the same.

For Joe and I and our kids, there is no greater joy than to see the legacy of faith in our family go down through the generations. I look back over the last almost 44 years and I know I've said it over and over again in these pages, but I have to say it again: I'm so grateful! God truly is *Forever Faithful.*

ABOUT THE AUTHOR

Stephanie Lombardo has been married to her high school sweetheart, Joseph, for 47 years. Together they have four, wonderful, grown kids and nine amazing grandchildren. They live in New Jersey, where they raised their family and attend Epic Church Intl. Since Stephanie became a believer in 1975, her heart has been to share the goodness and faithfulness of God wherever she goes.

Made in the USA
Monee, IL
27 May 2021

68844375R00069